THE EMPATHIC LEADER

An Effective Management Model for Enhancing Morale and Increasing Workplace Productivity

Dwayne L. Buckingham, Ph.D., LCSW, BCD

Other Great Books by Dr. Dwayne L. Buckingham

Resilient Thinking: The Power of Embracing Realistic and Optimistic Thoughts about Life, Love and Relationships

Qualified, Yet Single: Why Good Men Remain Single

A Phenomenological Study of the Experiences of Black Women

Can Black Women Achieve Marital Satisfaction? How Childhood Nurturing Experiences Impact Marital Happiness

Unconditional Love: What Every Woman and Man Desires in a Relationship

A Black Man's Worth: Conqueror and Head of Household

A Black Woman's Worth: My Queen and Backbone

Groundbreaking Films by Dr. Dwayne L. Buckingham

A Black Man's Worth: Conqueror and Head of Household

A Black Woman's Worth: My Queen and Backbone

Qualified, Yet Single: Why Good Men Remain Single

www.drbuckingham.com
www.realhorizonsdlb.com

THE EMPATHIC LEADER

An Effective Management Model for Enhancing Morale and Increasing Workplace Productivity

Dwayne L. Buckingham, Ph.D., LCSW, BCD

An Imprint of RHCS Publishing

The Empathic Leader

Copyright © 2014 by Dr. Dwayne L. Buckingham

Additional copies of this book can be purchased on-line at www.realhorizonsdlb.com or by contacting:

R.E.A.L. Horizons Consulting Service, LLC
P.O. Box 2665
Silver Spring, MD 20915
240-242-4087 Voice mail

ISBN: 9780985576523
Library of Congress Control Number: 2014907519
Edited by Verona Boucher
Cover Design by Dr. Dwayne L. Buckingham
For Worldwide Distribution
Printed in the United States of America

The Empathic Leader Icon

The Empathic Leader icon – a scroll with the word 'employee' placed on top – is a reminder that leaders should lead with a follower's perspective in mind. It also reminds each of us of the importance of putting ourselves in our employees' shoes so that we can consciously strive to understand the world through their perspective and never devalue them.

Dedication

To every manager who gives all that he or she can to inspire and develop productive and healthy employees in the workplace.

CONTENTS

Foreword

Richard P. Chiles, Ph.D.

Assistant Professor, Department of Psychology
Jackson State University

In recent years, discussions regarding what it means to be an effective leader have become more prevalent in boardrooms, academia and the general populace as organizations around the world continue to struggle to retain productive and happy employees. It is widely believed that effective leadership is about influencing individuals to achieve a common goal or outcome that will advance the organization. Leaders who embrace this perspective more often than not have a tendency to place a great of emphasis on gaining employee compliance through coercion, rewards and control and ultimately become obsessed with achieving organizational goals.

As a licensed psychologist and assistant professor with more than thirty-years of clinical and leadership experience, it is my belief that outcome-based leadership approaches are ineffective because leaders who use these styles often fail to nurture the human need to be validated, heard and most importantly understood.

The most effective leaders invest time in understanding their employees and developing relationships with them. This is critical to ensuring the success of the organization because employees are more likely to be responsive and accountable to leaders who care about their emotional well-being. If leaders spent time more bonding with employees, workplace environments would be more enjoyable. But sadly, a large percentage of leaders still feel that the workplace environment is not an appropriate setting to display empathy or any other emotion. For many, the work environment is considered to be a place to earn a paycheck. Given this widespread and one-sided thinking, increasing productivity takes precedence over enhancing morale and taking care of people.

Dr. Dwayne L. Buckingham in this enlightening book, *The Empathic Leader,* accurately captures the essence of what it means to be empathetic toward employees while achieving organizational goals. His personal transformation from being a mission-focused tyrant leader to a people-focused empathic leader provides a practical roadmap to success which all of us can appreciate. His transparent and humanistic approach to leadership inspires us to believe in the greatness that dwells within employees when leaders replace dominance with empathy.

I have had the privilege of mentoring and seeing the author effectively turn leadership and life challenges into successes. This book is not just about leadership; it's a blue-print for helping leaders develop meaningful and impactful relationships at work and beyond. *The Empathic Leader* is a personal testimony of the power of understanding and nurturing people's emotional well-being. It a triumph story about demonstrating compassion and its impact on organizational success.

I enjoyed reading this manuscript and encourage you to embrace and apply The 5 Skills of Highly Empathic Leaders and practical advice printed on these pages. This book will become a classic that is used by and shared among leaders from around the world. *The Empathic Leader* is predestined to join the list of best-selling books on leadership and will be used globally to develop people-centered and compassionate leaders. From CEOs to front-line supervisors, this book shows us how to lead with empathy and achieve organizational success by transforming ourselves, our employees and our organizations.

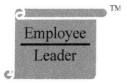

Employee / Leader ™

The Empathic Leader

Introduction

Empathic Leadership Can No Longer Be Optional

With an increase in workplace violence, burnout, job dissatisfaction and employee turnover, the demand for change in management styles has never been greater than it is today. The traditional hierarchical, dictatorial styles of leadership are a thing of the past. Tyrannical management has lost traction over the past few decades as people demand more empathically to be treated fairly in the workplace.

This parable *The Empathic Leader* is a short story that exemplifies the importance of demonstrating empathy by supporting and listening to people instead of being bossy and pushing them around. By reading this thought-provoking, heartfelt story, you will learn about the moral dilemmas I experienced and the lessons I learned on my journey toward becoming an empathic leader.

Through personal experience, I have learned that authoritative tactics and lack of empathy toward employees typically diminishes morale and productivity. Telling people what to do without considering how they feel or failing to solicit their input about performance improvement is counterproductive to effective leadership and organizational success.

For most employees, the need to be accepted, appreciated, cared about, trusted, respected, understood, valued, and supported are emotional needs that strongly influence how they will perform. I now recognize that my primary goal as a leader is to develop dynamic relationships with my employees so that they can feel safe enough to discuss their concerns with me.

This book is a guide to help you become an empathic leader. Given the leadership failures that are so prevalent today and the unfortunate increase in job dissatisfaction, employee turnover, burnout, suicide and workplace violence, a change in managerial style is no longer optional, and *Empathic Leadership* can help empower you to realize that change.

Most of the managers that I have coached approached me because they have recognized that if they are to enhance morale and increase productivity in their work environments, they must adopt the *Empathic Leadership* approach. *Empathic Leadership* is not dictating at all. Rather, it is about creating a positive and compassionate workplace where employees can perform exceptionally well.

As you implement the *Empathic Leadership* approach, remember that your workplace success can be determined by both process and outcome. Be patient, embrace the challenge, recognize and praise change, remain optimistic and don't forget that *Empathic Leadership* can no longer be optional.

I hope that you enjoy reading this book and that you will embrace The 5 Skills of Highly Empathic Leaders outlined within it. Are you ready? Here's my story:

^{TM}

Employee
Leader

Committed to
Leadership

Monday, July 27, 1998 changed my life forever. On this particular day, I not only became an American Airman, I also became a leader in one of the world's most powerful and dominant organizations. With my surrogate father and younger brother at my side, I walked into a small, scorching hot recruitment office in Jackson, Mississippi to take the oath to become a commissioned officer in the United States Air Force.

Being the first of eight children to attend and graduate from college was a significant milestone, but walking into that recruitment office and taking the oath to serve and defend this great country was one of the most humbling experiences in my life. As I stood smiling from ear to ear, I held my hand up with pride and recited the United States Uniformed Services Oath of Office:

I, Dwayne L. Buckingham, do solemnly swear that I will support and defend the Constitution of the United States against all enemies foreign and domestic; that I will bear true faith and allegiance to the same: that I take this obligation freely, without any mental reservation or purpose of evasion; and that I will well and faithfully discharge the duties of the office on which I am about to enter. So help me God.

What a moment! As I walked out of the recruitment office, I told myself that I would give 110 percent as a leader and do whatever is needed to accomplish the Air Force's mission. I entered that office as a proud citizen and exited as a proud First Lieutenant.

A few days after receiving my commission, I returned to my hometown of St. Louis, Missouri and began preparing to start a new career and lifestyle in the world's greatest air and space force. In preparation for my new venture, I developed a daily workout regimen that included waking up at 5 a.m. for a three-mile run followed by an intense two-hour weight-lifting routine. I did not know much about the military culture at that time, but from watching television commercials, I was convinced that "good leaders" were tough and strong. Also, in speaking with a few veterans, I was told that physical and mental discipline was honored and respected among the military ranks.

Excited to serve, I left St. Louis on August 1, 1998 and drove over 6 hours to Maxwell Air Force Base (AFB) in Alabama to attend Officer Training School (OTS). As I drove toward my future, I realized that my life would never be the same. I was embarking upon a journey that was filled with uncertainty. Several thoughts raced through my mind as I traveled south on that crowded highway. Will I be safe? Will I excel as a leader? Am I capable of sacrificing and giving my all? Will I miss my family? Am I truly willing and prepared to die defending my country?

My thoughts and feelings intensified as I reflected on the horror stories that I had heard from Vietnam veterans who witnessed unimaginable violence and came face to face with the ultimate sacrifice – death. With mixed emotions and a jumble of thoughts, I took a deep breath and reminded myself that everything would be fine because I had already been tested and had succeeded as a leader on the battlefield of life.

Growing up in a single parent household in the inner-city ghetto, witnessing extreme violence in my neighborhood, experiencing the brutal death of several loved ones and losing my mother to cancer at age 17 were just a few of the devastating trials and tribulations I had endured. Nevertheless, with a commitment to leadership and mission completion, I became the first of eight siblings to attend college and graduate with honors, the first in my entire family to earn a Master's degree, and the first to become an officer in the United States Armed Forces.

After engaging in this soul-searching revelation, my ambivalence faded and, at that moment, I decided to never question my decision to join the military or to lead others ever again, secure in the belief that I was born to lead.

A Leader in the Making

Upon my arrival at Gunter Annex located within the 23rd Training Squadron on Maxwell AFB, I was informed by one of the training instructors that I would be required to complete a four-week Commissioned Officer Training (COT) course prior to reporting to my operational unit or first duty station. During this initial brief, I learned that COT was designed to provide initial officership training to Air Force judge advocates, chaplains, health professionals and medical scholarship recipients who were awarded direct commission based on our professional credentials in our respective fields. I also learned that the primary purpose of COT was to produce motivated leaders who embodied the American warrior ethos. As I reviewed the curriculum, I was eager to learn why so much emphasis was placed on cultural competency and expeditionary thinking and readiness.

The first two weeks of training focused on team-building, followership and knowledge acquisition. Weeks three and four focused on leadership application. The program combined lectures, readings, guided discussions, classroom exercises, field leadership exercises and after-hours training activities to equip my colleagues and I with an in-depth understanding of our roles as Air Force commissioned officers.

Learning to become an officer and leader in the military environment was not an easy task. "Be tough and accomplish the mission" was a message that I heard regularly in the classroom and during training activities. It was not unusual for instructors to publicly correct or chastise trainees in order to let everyone know what was and was not acceptable behavior. Maintaining good discipline, order and accomplishing the mission appeared to be the most important aspects of becoming a "great" officer and leader. The ability to maintain order, think quickly and solve problems was highly praised and reinforced on a regular basis.

To test our ability to lead others, each trainee was tasked with leading an obstacle course and was evaluated on his or her ability to accomplish the mission. The pressure to succeed was intense, but the desire to please the instructors was even greater. Excuses were not allowed and instructors frequently reminded us that mission accomplishment was our primary objective. Those who accomplished the mission were praised and those who came up short were instructed to perform until they succeeded. Discussions about emotional distress did not happen in the classroom and definitely did not occur on the obstacle course. If one of us appeared to be under emotional distress, we were encouraged to suck it up and to remain focused on the mission.

During one of the obstacle drills, when one trainee appeared to be emotionally distraught, the instructor shouted without hesitation, "There is no place in the workplace for emotions! Consider this obstacle course your workplace. Emotions are distracting and cause people to lose focus. Get it together because other people depend on you. You have a job to do – complete the mission!"

Over the intense four-week training, I received thorough instruction in the areas of the profession of arms, military and regional studies, leadership, and communication skills. I also participated in over 40 hours of leadership practicum activities, including the Leadership Reaction Course, High Ropes Obstacle Course, and an emergency medical response exercise in an expeditionary environment.

Finally, after fulfilling all the requirements and passing my examination, I began preparing for graduation, and was again filled with excitement. I felt that I had truly embraced the spirit of officership – lead with honor and get the job done. I did not take my leadership position lightly and understood that I had to maintain a high standard of conduct because I had been charged with one of the greatest responsibilities of officership – developing Airmen who would achieve the Air Force's mission of flying, fighting and winning…. in air, space and cyberspace.

On graduation day the keynote speaker reminded us that we should always take care of our people, but encouraged us to never compromise the mission. As he approached the end of his speech, he stated, "The American people sleep well at night because you and I have agreed to give our lives to protect them. If needed, we will drop massive bombs and kill all enemies who pose a threat to our nation's safety and freedom. You are this nation's future leadership and I know that you all are up for the task. I am confident that you will make our country proud. As you report to your various operational units around the world, keep the mission and core values of integrity first; service before self; and excellence in all we do in the forefront of your mind, and you will succeed in advancing your unit and organization to the next level. I look forward to serving with you and would like to thank each of you again for your willingness to defend this great country."

And so began a lifelong exploration of leadership, one that has shaped me personally and professionally.

Mission and Results
Focused

It was a pleasant and sunny day when I arrived in Panama City, a small town that is often referred to as "L.A. or Lower Alabama." With less than one month as a leader in the military, I had successfully accomplished my first mission – arriving safely at Tyndall Air Force Base, my first operational unit.

As I approached the secured gate, a sudden sharp feeling of anxiety rushed through my body. With my Permanent Change of Station (PCS) orders in hand, I slowly pulled toward the guardsmen on duty. One of the young airmen causally moved toward my vehicle and asked for identification. After carefully reviewing my I.D. and orders, he provided directions to the in-processing office and saluted me. I returned the salute, drove off and proceeded in the direction of the processing office.

Upon entering the processing office, I was greeted by my supervisor, Major Robert Cook. With a warm smile on his face, he firmly shook my hand and welcomed me to the Air Force.

My initial impression of Major Cook was very positive. He appeared to be a down-to-earth guy who was easy to interact with. This was very refreshing as my previous interactions with higher ranking training instructors in OTS were extremely intense.

Major Cook and I briefly talked about my trip to Tyndall and then he escorted me to officer lodging where I secured a room. After I finished checking in and unpacking a few items,

Major Cook welcomed me a second time and directed me to report to work at 0730 hrs as he departed the room.

I replied, "Yes sir," and thanked him for his generosity. With the evening coming to an end, I turned off the television and got in bed. As I lay there, I remember thinking, *"This is it! I am about to be put to the test. How will I do as a leader? Will I accomplish the mission and get results?"*

The Family Advocacy Program

When I reported to work the next morning, Major Cook was standing in front of the Family Advocacy building and gestured for me to follow him to his large and spacious office located in the middle of the building.

Upon entering his office, Major Cook invited me to sit down on his couch and proceeded to ask, "How much do you know about your job?"

Caught slightly off guard by his directness, I replied, "Sir, I was told that I will function as the Family Advocacy Officer and will be responsible for administering the Family Advocacy Program."

Major Cook responded, "Are you up for the challenge? Of all the highly visible family center programs on base, the Family Advocacy Program is among the top ten. With an emphasis on the prevention and treatment of child and spouse maltreatment, the program is a vital resource for leadership, service members and their dependents.

"Not only will you be responsible for overseeing and providing case management and treatment for all eligible beneficiaries," he continued, "you will also be responsible for ensuring wartime and combat capability of all airmen who utilize family advocacy services. This is a very intense program."

I took a deep breath and responded. "Sir, yes I am up for the challenge and have confidence that I will succeed at administering the program."

"Good. I need a confident and strong leader who can run this program," said Major Cook.

"Sir is there any advice or suggestions that you can offer that will help me successfully manage the program?"

With a smile on his face, he said, "I am glad that you asked. I would advise you to continue to ask questions. Performing in this highly visible position can be very stressful at times and you should seek guidance whenever you feel challenged. I do not expect you to do everything right, but I do expect you to give your best, seek guidance and remain committed to accomplishing the mission."

"Thank you Sir, I will definitely seek guidance when warranted. I appreciate your willingness to mentor and guide me as I move forward in performing my responsibilities as a junior officer and leader. I will try not to bother you too much."

"Providing guidance is part of my responsibility as Flight Commander, plus I take pride in mentoring, listening to and trying to understand the people I lead," answered Major Cook.

With a sigh of relief, I stated, "Sir, your leadership approach appears to be slightly different than what I was exposed to during OTS. You appear to be more concerned about and in tune with taking care of people."

"Yes!" Major Cook said as he walked toward his office window. "Empathy is an indispensable leadership skill. When interacting with staff, I try to put myself in their shoes because I believe that it is impossible to connect with or motivate anyone, especially employees if I cannot envision what work or life would be like if I walked in their shoes. I consider myself to be an *Empathic Leader*. I manage my staff by practicing the 5 Skills of Highly Empathic Leaders. Application of the five skills helps me enhance employee morale and increase their productivity. You will learn more about my approach and the skills overtime. Trust me, we will have many conversations about leadership. If you ever need guidance about how to manage staff, please do not hesitate to come back and see me. But for now I want you to focus on managing the Family Advocacy Program and getting to know your staff."

"Due to the intense nature of the Family Advocacy Program, four highly experienced civilian employees were hired to provide case management, treatment and outreach services for eligible beneficiaries. Also, three enlisted personnel were assigned to the program as well."

With an appreciative smile on my face I replied, "Thank you Sir," and exited the office.

Thrilled about meeting my staff, I immediately walked to my office and sent an email informing them that I wanted to have a one hour meet and greet meeting at 0730 hrs the next day so that I could get to know them.

Getting to Know Staff

At 0715 hrs, I entered the conference room where all staff meetings were held and to my surprise, I found all the staff seated and ready to talk. As I took my seat, I thanked everyone for arriving early and introduced myself, speaking briefly about my professional background and my reason for joining the military.

After I finished speaking, I asked each of them to introduce themselves and to tell me their roles in the program. Without hesitation, Joe introduced himself first. "Hi, I am Joe. I have been in the social work field for over 20 years. Prior to taking this job as treatment manager, I worked as an active duty social worker in the Army. I retired two years ago. I enjoy doing clinical work with families and do a lot of cognitive-behavioral therapy."

"Nice to meet you," I replied.

Rhonda followed. "Hi, I'm Rhonda. Most people describe me as a very energetic, fun and pleasant person. I have been in the social work field for 15 years and I really enjoy working as a treatment manager. I provide individual and couples therapy. I have been working in this program for the past seven years."

"Are you the life of the party around here?" I asked.

"Yes sir that is me!" commented Rhonda.

After looking around the room, Sara smiled and stated, "It is nice to meet you and I look forward to working with you. I am a registered nurse with more than 20 years of experience. I retired from the Air Force five years ago and enjoy working the Home-Based Opportunities Make Everyone Successful (HOMES) Program for families at risk for maltreatment."

"Hi, I'm Jill. I am the Family Advocacy outreach manager and I have been working in this position for the past two years. Like the others, I enjoy my job and take pride in providing educational information to families. I, too, am a social worker and have over 12 years of experience."

"Hi sir, I am Erica. I work in the front office as the administrative assistant. I will be scheduling and managing your patient appointments and all meetings. I have been with the program for two years."

"Hi sir," the next individual began, "I am Airman Jackson and I joined the Air Force less than eight months ago and this is my first duty station. I enjoy working in the program, but I have a lot to learn."

"Good morning Sir, I am Staff Sergeant James. I enlisted in the Army five years ago and I am assigned to Fort Bragg in North Carolina. However, due to a staffing shortage, I have been temporarily detailed to work in FAP as the Non-Commissioned Officer in Charge (NCOIC). I am responsible for making sure the office runs smoothly and look forward to serving with you."

"Good morning Sir, I am Tech Sergeant Williams. I enlisted in the Air Force 10 years ago and I am responsible for ensuring that the Mental Health Flight runs smoothly. I primarily provide guidance to the junior enlisted personnel and serve as the Senior Enlisted Advisor for you and the Flight Commander."

At the conclusion of the staff introductions, I thanked each of them and informed them that I was looking forward to serving and working with them, adding that I felt blessed to have this wonderful opportunity to work with such experienced and dedicated people.

Prior to ending the meet and greet, I ask Erica to touch base with each staff member in order to schedule one-to-one meetings with me so that I could get to know them a little better and also to discuss my expectations.

"Roger that Sir," said Erica with a smile.

Mission First or People First

With less than one week on the job, I decided to hold 30-minute one-to-one meetings with staff to review and discuss my expectations. As the supervisor, I felt that it was a good idea to go over my expectations upfront so that everybody would know what their responsibilities were and also know what they would be held accountable for.

As each employee entered my office I asked him or her to have a seat and stated, "In order to accomplish the mission and to create a productive work environment it is important that everyone understand what is expected of him or her. As your new Family Advocacy Officer (FAO), I am charged with the task of not only holding everyone accountable for their work and actions, but to ensure that we provide excellent care to service members and their families."

I spent the remaining time discussing my expectations and requested my employees to sign the form acknowledging that they understood what was expected of them. Despite the fact that one of the staff members refused to sign the form because she did not like my approach, I thought the meetings went well overall.

"Mission accomplished," I thought.

Over the next few weeks, I walked around the office and talked with employees about performing efficiently and completing tasks in a timely manner.

My mission-focused approach worked well for me because I was very busy and personally did not feel a need to develop casual relationships at work. It was not uncommon for employees to hear me say, "There is no place in the workplace for emotions. We all have a job to do."

I wanted my staff to know that I was dedicated to achieving the mission and would hold them accountable for producing results. I noticed that staff rarely stopped by my office or approached me as I walked the hallways, but I was not bothered because I operated under the premise that I was at work to work and not to develop relationships with my employees.

As long as my staff provided excellent treatment, facilitated outreach education and did what was required of them, I was satisfied. With the exception of a few late reports, improperly formatted meeting minutes, and the absence of my signature block from a few important memos, I did not notice a significant decrease in performance. I informed staff about the minor errors and carried on with business as usual.

Four weeks passed and everything appeared to be going well. Then one day, out of the blue, Major Cook called me into his office. As I entered, he was sitting behind his desk, looking somewhat disappointed. "Lt Buckingham, you have a problem with your staff and we have to talk about it. Remember that I told you that we will have many conversations about my leadership approach; well, consider this conversation number one."

Startled, I asked, "Sir, what is the problem?"

"Several of your staff members stopped by my office last week and complained about your leadership style. They reported that you have been rigid, unfair and difficult to work with. They also reported that you are obsessed with achieving the mission and had each of them sign a form outlining your expectations. As I allowed them to vent, they ranted about how you have not scheduled anytime to get to know them personally."

As I listened, I felt my blood pressure rising. I was angered because my staff had crucified me for doing my job. I was also angered by the fact that they went behind by back and spoke with my boss without informing me.

Sensing my frustration, Major Cook said, "Calm down. I know you are offended and probably think that you are in trouble with me. You are not in any trouble, but I am going to take this opportunity to educate you about the first skill of *Highly Empathic Leaders*."

Major Cook walked from behind his desk and said, "You have a serious dilemma, and I am going to present you with two options to help you solve it. Option #1 – Remain angered: reprimand your staff and ignore their complaints; or Option #2 – Lead in a Righteous Manner: manage your employees with integrity, good intentions and dignity which means that you do right by them and treat them how you would like to be treated. The choice is yours, but I highly recommend that you chose the option that is more likely to enhance morale and increase productivity."

After he finished informing me about my options, I looked at him and said, "Sir, thanks for offering solutions, but you said that you were going to take this opportunity to educate me about the first skill that is practiced by *Highly Empathic Leaders*."

Major Cook laughed and said, "I just did. Option #2 is the first skill."

With a puzzled look, I asked, "What do you mean Sir?"

"**Leading in a Righteous Manner** means that you should always do right by your employees. Empathic leaders lead by applying the Golden Rule, which states that, 'One should treat others as one would like others to treat oneself.' With this in mind, an empathic leader consistently strives to treat all employees how he or she would like to be treated. As a young and mission-focused manager like you, I used to always put the mission before people. However, as I matured as a leader over the course of my fifteen-year career, I have learned that bonding with employees is the key to enhancing morale and increasing productivity. Connecting with staff is very important. Even if I do not always agree with what they have to say, I always listen. By demonstrating this effortless professional courtesy, I have successfully developed respectful and trusting relationships with all of my employees."

Still upset, I replied, "Sir, why should I be thoughtful or considerate of them or their emotions? They did not consider my feelings when they came to you. They are a bunch of backstabbers and I feel betrayed."

In a sympathetic tone, Major Cook replied, "You cannot allow your negative emotions to get the best of you and prevent you from doing the right thing. Empathy is one of the most important interpersonal skills you can demonstrate toward people because you will learn the importance of open-mindedness, sharing and being transparent. I know this is difficult for you to understand now, but I highly recommend that you schedule a meeting and listen to them. Treat them how you would like to be treated. It's the right thing to do."

After Major Cook stopped speaking, I glanced at him and said, "Sir, I respect what you are saying, but I do not understand why I have to address their emotional issues. What does all this have to do with achieving the mission?"

"I understand your confusion," Major Cook replied. "I did not get it first either, but hear me out. Your ability to enhance employee morale and increase productivity begins with you, and leadership is vital to those objectives. *Empathic Leadership* is a process-oriented communication skill that is learned through a combination of education, training and practice. The primary goal is to gain a deeper understanding of others' emotions and perspectives in order to identify, discuss and resolve emotional distress that may cause or contribute to low morale and productivity. If you do not listen to or get anything else that I tell you from this point on, please get this: *Lead in a Righteous Manner.* Without successful application of this first skill, the remaining four skills cannot be implemented or applied successfully."

"What are the other four skills?" I inquired.

"In time, I will educate you about the other four skills, but for now I need you to focus on the first skill," Major Cook said.

"Thank you Sir! I appreciate the guidance and will schedule the meeting."

As we walked toward the door, Major Cook looked at me with an encouraging smile and whispered, "After you conduct the meeting, come back and tell me what happened."

As I stood in the hallway, I felt tremendously confused and anxious. I understood exactly what I needed to do, but dreaded the thought of doing it. Leading in a righteous manner sounded very simple from a logical standpoint, but emotionally, I was struggling to embrace the skill.

Anxious and uncertain, one thought ran through my mind, *"Doing right by others when you perceive that they have wronged you is not easy."*

I quickly gathered myself and refocused, reminding myself that I had a mission to complete. Although I was not at peace with what was being asked of me, Major Cook's instruction was clear:

Lead in a Righteous Manner
Manage with integrity, good intentions and dignity: do right by your employees and treat them how you would like to be treated.

Over the next few days, I tried to imagine how I would start and end the dreaded meeting. Major Cook had suggested that I schedule a meeting, but did not tell me what to do or say. For the first time since joining the military, I felt unprepared to accomplish the mission.

I reflected on how unpreparedness increased my anxiety and I thought, "I am prepared and willing to die for my country, but I am extremely anxious about talking to my staff about their emotions."

This simple but necessary task was more difficult for me than I wanted to acknowledge. I was effective at ensuring task completion, but had not yet developed the skill or confidence needed to respond to my staff's emotional needs. At that moment, I felt extremely ineffective as a leader.

Then, one Sunday night, while lying restless in bed, I began to think deeply about why I was commissioned to be a leader in the military. I quickly realized that I was granted this awesome privilege based on my expertise as a clinical social worker and ability to take care of people.

Although the latter was obvious, I had lost sight of this basic fact because I had been told on numerous occasions that I was an officer first and a clinical social worker second. Given this, I spent the majority of my time trying to become an effective officer and rarely used the conflict resolution skills that I possessed as a clinician. Just then, it hit me, *"Caring for people is as equally important as leading them. One without the other will not yield good results."* This timely revelation left me feeling refreshed, relaxed and empowered. I started thinking about what I would do and say to a group of distressed employees who felt misunderstood or wronged. Several thoughts surfaced all at once and in an attempt to capture all of them, I opened up my nightstand, pulled out my voice recorder and began speaking:

1. Listen to understand them and not to rebut
2. Listen with an objective ear
3. Demonstrate empathy: how would I feel if I was in their place?
4. Apologize – say I am sorry and let them know that I care about their well-being

With midnight approaching, I turned off the audio recorder, jumped out of bed, kneeled and began to pray. "God give me the strength to do right by my staff. Please help me keep my pride in check so that I can listen with a compassionate heart and identify solutions that will create harmony in the workplace. I know that I will not always do the right thing, but

I ask that you help me remain mindful of the importance of treating others justly. Amen."

As I leaped back into bed and leaned over to cut off the nightlight, I quietly spoke, *"I can do this. All I have to do is to remember that everyone deserves an opportunity and the right to be heard, understood and treated fairly. Listen intensely and respond with a compassionate heart."*

Smiling and feeling inspired, I uttered, *"Good night!"* to myself and peacefully fell asleep.

The Dreaded Staff Meeting

At approximately 0800 hrs on Monday morning, staff entered the meeting room and took their seats around the table. After they settled in, I informed them that we would not be following our regular agenda. As I glanced around the silent room, I felt my anxiety increasing, so I took a deep breath and began, "I have learned a lot about myself over the past few weeks and have come to understand that I have unintentionally created a hostile work environment. A few weeks ago Major Cook called me into his office and informed me that some of you were unhappy with my leadership style. He stated that several individuals approached him and reported that they did not like my mission-focused approach to management. He also stated that individuals complained about my impersonal day-to-day mannerism as a leader.

"Initially, I was very angry and offended by the accusations. I felt betrayed. However, I took some time to process and I am in a better place now. I decided the best way to address complaints is to have a heart-to-heart talk with you all and that is the purpose for today's meeting. I want to hear from you all and I promise that no one will be reprimanded for speaking up. My intent is to walk out of this room as a harmonious and unified team, so please speak up. In order to make sure that I hear what is said, I will listen to everyone before I say anything."

Joe, the outspoken and straightforward treatment manager, was the first to speak. He looked me directly in my eyes and said, "I respect and admire your dedication toward accomplishing the mission, but I do not like your method. You spend a great deal of time focusing on productivity, but have never once asked me or others how we are doing. I have worked with dozens of managers prior to retiring from the military and I can tell you that those who primarily focus on results rarely gained the respect and trust of their employees. Getting the job done is important, but I would ask that you take some time to get to know us."

As Joe finished, I thought, *"What have I done? The flood gates have been opened!"*

Sara, the lighthearted nurse, spoke next. "You are very smart and competent, but you are not the easiest person to get along with. Since you arrived, the thought of resigning has crossed my mind several times. I work very hard, but do not feel appreciated. The more I do, the more you demand. I know that I have a job to do and also know that I will get paid to do it; however, a little appreciation would be nice. You don't smile much. Please lighten up."

A few other employees shared their thoughts and concerns about my leadership approach and by the time they all finished, I was feeling really low. However, I maintained my composure, gathered my thoughts and responded as such, "I truly appreciate everyone for speaking up. Obviously it was hard for me to hear what was said, but I believe that transparency and honesty is important to developing a healthy work environment.

"I chose not to respond until after everyone spoke because I did not want anyone to feel like I was refuting their thoughts or feelings. I simply wanted to listen and I am glad that you all spoke up because I now have a better understanding of how you all feel. In listening intensely, I picked up on a few themes. You want to be appreciated, understood, respected and treated like human beings and not robots working on an assembly line, correct?"

"Yes!" Nancy shouted, followed by Joe, who exclaimed, "Yes Sir, you got it!"

Smiling, I stated, "I can relate. I do not believe that I would be happy or satisfied either if I had to work for a manager who was mission-focused and not personable. If I could rewind the hands of time, I would, but because I cannot I hope that all of you accept my apology. I am sorry! I truly do care about how you all feel and from this point on I will be more attentive. Please feel free to approach me whenever there is a need. I will make myself available.

"As I call this meeting to an end, is there anything else that anyone would like to say?"

"Yes," replied Rhonda. "I would like to thank you for listening to us. This meeting was very helpful and productive because I now feel much better about approaching you. I now believe and trust that you have our best interest in mind. I cannot speak for others, but from this point on I will do my best to help you succeed as a leader."

As I got up from my seat, I thanked Rhonda for believing in me and offering to help me succeed. As I moved toward the door, several staff members thanked me as well, shook my hand and walked away smiling.

As the dreaded meeting had come to an end, I felt relieved as a result of achieving my goals, which were: to listen to understand and not rebut, listen with an objective ear, to demonstrate empathy and to apologize.

I was floating on cloud nine because I had successfully implemented and applied the first skill commonly practiced by *Highly Empathic Leaders:*

Lead in a Righteous Manner

The Debrief

Around 1300 hrs I stopped by Major Cook's office to brief him about my staff meeting. As I entered the office, Major Cook asked, "How did it go?"

I smiled and said, "You were right, Sir! I did exactly what you told me – *Lead in a Righteous Manner* and it worked. Listening to my staff was the right thing to do. I did not understand the importance of listening to disgruntled employees, but now I do. If I would have reprimanded them or ignored how they felt, things would have only gotten worse."

"By listening to them, demonstrating empathy and expressing concern, I was able to gain their trust and respect."

"I am glad you get it," replied Major Cook. He walked toward me, shook my hand and continued, "Never forget that how employees feel does matter. Employees who feel misunderstood, unappreciated or disrespected often perform in a substandard manner and are more likely to engage in passive/aggressive behavior. Authoritative tactics and lack of empathy for employees typically set the stage for low morale and decreased productivity.

"Morale is associated with employees' emotions, attitudes and satisfaction levels, while productivity is associated with employees' workplace output. Morale is an emotional reaction. It is a subjective and qualitative workplace factor that is understood by examining employees' feelings and perceptions about their workplace environment. Productivity, on the other hand, is an objective and quantitative workplace factor that is best understood by examining employees' service completion or product distribution.

"Morale and productivity are often spoken of as being two different workplace factors that impact organizational success, but they are one in the same and need to be addressed simultaneously. Research has shown that employee morale is directly linked to productivity. Many human relations experts insist that unhappy and dissatisfied employees are less productive than happy and satisfied employees."

Glowing from within, I said, "You're right Sir. I truly get it now! My success as a leader rests not only on my ability to learn and apply mission-focused strategies to get results but on my ability to correctly analyze the underlying cause of employees' low morale and productivity. By understanding how employees think and feel, I will be able to provide them with the resources and support they need to succeed in the workplace. If I preach that my employees are my greatest resource, then I have to treat them as such. *Empathic Leadership* is treating employees with empathy and respect to maximize their productivity. It is listening and supporting them rather than instructing and controlling them."

"Correct!" Major Cook confirmed. "As a leader, you are charged with the responsibility of mentoring, coaching and supporting your employees. It is irrational to expect employees to check their emotions at the door prior to entering the workplace. Emotions are linked to relationships and *Empathic Leaders* understand that their ability to produce great results is strongly influenced by their ability to develop quality relationships with their people."

"As you *Lead in a Righteous Manner*, remember that you will continue to be confronted with morale and productivity issues. However, as long as you treat people how you would like to be treated, your ability to resolve them will come with ease."

"So, if applying this simple skill will help enhance morale and productivity, why is it so difficult for managers to execute?" I asked.

Major Cook smiled and said, "Unfortunately, many organizations are led by leaders who earned their managerial positions through diligence, hard work, mission dedication and technical efficiency. And although these skills are vital for functioning and succeeding in management, they do not always contribute to the development of a positive workplace culture. Furthermore, executives spend millions of dollars developing and implementing performance-focused training programs or sending managers to seminars that are designed to equip them with technical and intellectual information needed to motivate employees to perform well and to meet deliverables."

He continued, "Leading righteously is one of the most important interpersonal components of building a positive workplace. It is a process-oriented and self-reflection skill that is learned through a combination of training and practice. And yes, you are correct. The skill is simple. However, some managers lack the skill set and others are too busy to practice it."

"I appreciate the information, sir!"

"Do you mind if I record my thoughts about what I just learned before I forget?" I asked.

"Go right ahead, I think you should record everything that you learn about *Empathic Leadership.* We are just getting started. I have yet to inform you about the other four skills," Major Cook said.

I pulled out my pocket recorder and began speaking.

Leading in a Righteous Manner has several benefits:

1. Employees feel respected
2. Employees feel understood
3. Employees feel valued
4. Employees can achieve greater professional satisfaction
5. Employees will look out for, protect and support their leader

"You are right on target," Major Cook exclaimed, "You're on your way to becoming an *Empathic Leader.*"

"I appreciate it, sir!" I responded. "What are the other four skills of *Highly Empathic Leaders?*"

He rose from his seat and said, "Let's take a tour through the hospital and I will tell you about the other four skills as we walk about. As we walk the hallways, I want you to pay attention to the interactions between staff and customers. Also, I want you to pay attention to signs hanging on doors and walls throughout the hospital."

"Yes sir," I replied.

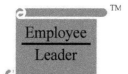

The Hospital Tour

A s Major Cook gathered his belongings, I thought, *"How is a trip through the hospital going to help me learn about the other four skills?"*

Despite my skepticism, I was still excited. I thought, "Take advantage of every opportunity to learn about leadership. After all, walking around the hospital is good exercise and can do no harm."

Major Cook and I got on the elevator and road to the fifth floor. From there, we turned down the hall and walked into the Equal Employment Opportunity Office.

Equal Employment Opportunity Office (EEO)

As I walked into the office behind Major Cook, I noticed that there were several signs about discrimination and fairness hanging on the doors and walls. Major Cook observed the uncertain look on my face and asked, "You probably are wondering why I brought you to EEO."

"Yes sir, the question crossed my mind," I replied.

"Here is your answer." Major Cook handed me an EEO brochure and said, "Read the purpose statement."

I read:

"The purpose of equal employment opportunity (EEO) is to ensure fairness in hiring, promotion and other workplace practices. Ultimately, this will encourage a diverse, multi-talented workforce."

After I finished reading the brochure, Major Cook asked, "Which words in the purpose statement stood out to you and why?"

I thought for a second. "I guess *fairness, diverse, and multi-talented*. If organizations are to succeed during these very competitive times, they must treat employees fairly and hire from a diverse pool of people who have different talents."

"Yes," he agreed. "When I first read the brochure, I also focused on *fairness, diverse* and *multi-talented*. I believe that people will perform well if they are treated fairly and are respected for the talent that they bring to the organization." He walked into the waiting area and said, "Come in here, Lt Buckingham."

He pointed toward a sign on the wall and asked, "What does the sign on the wall say? Highly empathic leaders practice it often."

"*Appreciate Diversity and Respect Differences,*" I answered. "Is this the second skill of Highly Empathic Leaders?" I asked.

"No, it isn't." Major Cook commented. "However, the sign reminds us of the importance of recognizing and appreciating individuality and respecting differences. One of the most challenging aspects of leadership is learning not to judge or compare employees. To overcome this challenge, we must **Suspend Judgment** that is the second skill to becoming an *Empathic Leader*. Suspending judgment requires us to monitor biases and celebrate individuality by being flexible in our thinking. It is the second most important skill because it empowers leaders to create an environment built on mutual trust and respect. If employees feel that judgment will be passed on them, communication will not occur or will end immediately after it begins. Furthermore, suspending judgment is important because it enables leaders to engage employees with an open mind and clear conscience."

Then he turned to me and asked, "Do you understand the importance of Skill 2 – Suspend Judgment? This skill is very important. Without successful comprehension and implementation of Skill 2, the Empathic Leadership process ends immediately."

"Yes," I replied. "It's the same skill that I apply when interacting with clients in the therapeutic setting. As a clinical social worker I have an ethical obligation to respect the inherent dignity and worth of all individuals. Like others, I have preconceived images and perceptions about people. However, I take time to learn about people so that I can develop a better understanding of what they need and how to interact with them."

"I knew you could relate from a personal and clinical perspective," said Major Cook, "But do you apply the skill when interacting with your employees?"

With a disappointed look, I responded, "No sir, not often. I know that I should suspend judgment when interacting with employees, but I am not as mindful."

"Don't be too hard on yourself. Unfortunately, this is not uncommon behavior," said Major Cook. "With pressure to get the most out of employees, many of us overlook how we treat them or to how they feel. Sometimes we can be very closed-minded and judgmental and not be aware."

He continued, "It is not uncommon for managers to focus on expressing appreciation for customer diversity, but spend little time expressing appreciation for employee diversity. Suspending judgment begins by respecting individuality on all levels. Employees should not be viewed or treated any different than customers when it comes to suspending judgment. They also have a right to think, act and perform differently. Different does not mean that one employee is better, or more committed than the other; it simply means he or she is different."

"Thanks for the reminder, Sir. Sometimes I forget to apply the simplest, but most important things. Employee differences should be viewed as assets. Managers should appreciate and recognize employees for their different work habits, different ways of communicating, different ways of learning, different ways of making decisions and different ways of completing tasks. If I get what you are saying, the best way to demonstrate appreciation and recognition is to *Suspend Judgment*."

"You're welcome and you are also correct." Major Cook said. "Now, are you ready to continue on our journey?"

"Yes Sir, but I need a few minutes to summarize what I just learned about Skill 2 – Suspend Judgment."

Major Cook looked at me and said, "Take your time. I want you to retain everything that you learn."

I pulled out my pocket recorder and began speaking.

Suspend Judgment has several benefits:

1. Encourages honest and open communication
2. Minimizes harmful competitiveness among employees
3. Increases awareness of and respect for individuality
4. Teaches employees to value and respect each other
5. Contributes to the development of a positive work environment

After I finished recording, I placed the recorder back into my pocket and asked, "Where are we going next, Sir?"

Major Cook appeared to be delighted by my enthusiasm and said, "I'm here to serve. Customer Service is our next stop. It's on the other end of the building."

Customer Service Department

As Major Cook and I walked down the long hallway toward customer service, he asked, "What do you think about your tour thus far?"

"To be honest, I did not believe that I would learn anything by walking around the hospital, but I guess I was wrong. Our trip to the EEO office was very enlightening."

"Good to hear," Major Cook commented. "After we walk into Customer Service, I want you to approach the representative and ask her to explain her role to you."

As we entered the Customer Service office, I said, "Good morning" and introduced myself to the representative seated at the front desk.

The lady smiled warmly and replied, "Good evening Sir" as she turned to give me her full attention. "How can I help you today?"

"I am curious about what you do and I am wondering if you could explain your role as a customer service representative."

"Is that it?" the lady replied. "I can definitely do that. Would you also like to receive handouts or brochures about our services?"

"Yes, please if you do not mind," I responded.

As the lady gathered information she began,

"My primary responsibility is to provide excellent customer service. I am here to comfort and help customers who experience any form of emotional distress."

"When customers approach my desk, I try to figure out the best way to help them. Initially, I do not spend as much time focusing on the cause of their distress. I have learned that people want to be comforted when they are upset so I do not get into heavy conversations about why they are upset. Also, I avoid lecturing them about policy. In the past, I would offer solutions instead of trying to understand customers' emotional distress and it never worked because they typically escalated," the lady concluded.

I smiled and thanked the lady for sharing.

Reflecting on what I had just heard, I turned toward Major Cook and said, "I understand the importance of providing good customer service, but what does good customer service have to do with being an *Empathic Leader* and managing employees?"

Major Cook grinned. "The customer service representative just educated you about the third skill that Highly Empathic Leaders apply which is to **Seek to Understand Employees** before responding or offering solutions. According to the hospital's customer service policy, is it ever appropriate to debate with or lecture customers who are emotionally distraught?"

"No, no and no," I echoed.

"You are correct," said Major Cook. "So why do we as managers fail to extend this same consideration to employees?"

I shrugged my shoulders and smiled as I replied, "I am not sure, Sir. Maybe we need to develop a policy."

Major Cook laughed and said, "Maybe we do need to develop a policy because premature problem-solving can cause employees to feel that we are more concerned with "fixing" them than we are with helping them. When employees are in emotional distress, they need support, not a lecture."

"Sir, I never thought about applying customer service skills when dealing with employees, but it makes sense. As the young lady stated, 'failure to understand emotional distress will often lead to escalation.' Relieving emotional distress should be first priority because nobody processes well when they are extremely emotional. By taking the time to understand an employee's emotional distress, we can help them identify healthier ways of viewing and dealing with their situation."

"I agree, but unfortunately, we do not always practice the obvious," Major Cook responded softly. "Being positive and demonstrating a caring attitude can make a big difference in relieving emotional distress."

"What is the best way to demonstrate a caring attitude?" I asked.

"First," Major Cook said, "Managers can begin by simply asking open-ended questions that stimulate dialogue. Two-way communication can increase self-awareness and responsibility. For example, a manager could start the conversation by asking, 'What are you feeling?' and follow up with, 'What steps can we take to help you feel better?'"

Feeling inspired, I whispered, "Sir, this is good stuff."

He chuckled and slowly turned to walk out of the Customer Service Department. As he approached the door, he stopped and asked, "You need me to wait a few minutes so that you can record what you just learned about Skill 3, correct?"

"Yes Sir." I pulled out my pocket recorder and began speaking.

Seek to Understand Employees has several benefits:

1. Demonstrates compassion for employees
2. Can prevent negative employee behavior from escalating
3. Better prepares leaders to help employees
4. Enhances leaders' questioning and listening skills
5. Helps employees develop a favorable impression of their leaders

After I finished recording, Major Cook said, "You are a smart guy and I am glad that you are enjoying your tour."

I smiled and said, "Thank you, Sir. I am definitely enjoying my tour. Where's the next stop?"

"I have taken hundreds of young managers on this tour over the past ten years and you are by far the most enthusiastic."

I looked at Major Cook and said, "Sir, I am committed to doing right by my employees. The more that I learn, the more I am realizing that organizational success is a by-product of employee satisfaction. I truly get the importance of what you are teaching me. Where are we headed next?"

"The Inspector General's Office," answered Major Cook. "You will learn about the fourth skill that *Highly Empathic Leaders* possess during our stop there."

The Inspector General's Office

When we arrived at the IG office, I noticed a sign on the exterior door that read, *"We Will Listen."* As we entered the office, I noticed another sign that read, *"We Investigate All Complaints."*

Major Cook noticed the two signs as well and asked, "What are your thoughts?"

"The signs say a lot," I commented. "When people visit the IG office they are either being investigated or are filing a complaint against someone else. Regardless of the reason for the visit, they are usually experiencing some kind of distress and are in need of support. They are looking to be heard. The signs say, 'We are here for you, so come on in.'"

"Yes," Major Cook agreed. "IG investigators examine various kinds of complaints and begin their process by doing what?"

"Engaging in reflective listening," I said. "They typically gather information and reflect back what they hear to make sure that they have recorded accurately."

"Yes," he said. "Reflective listening is a good communication skill to possess, but it has limitations."

"What do you mean?" I asked.

"Well, reflective listening requires the listener to identify what the speaker is feeling and then reflect understanding in an empathetic tone or manner. The primary purpose of reflective listening is to demonstrate that the listener understands how the speaker feels. Reflective listening works well unless the speaker is extremely emotional or is angry with the listener."

"Suppose one of your employees walked into your office and said, 'People around here just do not respect others. I asked the administrative assistant a question about some supplies I ordered last week and she ignored me. I am sick and tired of this damn place.' How would you respond?" asked Major Cook.

"I would say, 'You are very upset and frustrated because you were ignored. You would like people to be more respectful.'"

"Good response! Acknowledging emotions is a form of reflective listening. However, some people reject empathetic listening when they are upset. When people are upset they do not process well."

"I think I understand what you mean, Sir," I said. "Simply reflecting back what someone said in an empathetic tone is not always sufficient. People want to know if their feelings make sense to others. For example, I could respond by saying, 'If I was ignored I would feel frustrated as well. I can relate to how you feel and believe that most people would feel the same way if they were disrespected.' In addition to engaging in reflective listening, we have to also verbally express our understanding in an empathetic manner that communicates that we are emotionally aligned."

"Correct!" Major Cook said. "We have to learn how to communicate empathy by expressing it through our words. We have to send a message that says, 'I get how you feel and it's okay.' It is important to send such a message because it is extremely difficult to help someone calm down when he or she believe that you cannot relate to how he or she feels."

While listening intently I thought, *What does reflective listening have to do with Empathic Leadership.*"

Major Cook continued, "The fourth skill of *Highly Empathic Leaders* is not taught in many leadership courses or seminars, but is an essential communication skill. The technique is not foreign to you. You practice it daily in therapy as a clinician. What skill do you think managers need to possess in order to help employees feel comfortable enough to disclose their emotional distress?"

Smiling, I looked at Major Cook and said, "*Validation.*"

"You're right. Acknowledging employees' subjective experiences is critical to dismantling power struggles, resolving arguments and building genuinely trusting relationships."

"So I guess, *Acknowledgement of Subjective Experiences* is the fourth skill that is practiced by *Highly Empathic Leaders?*" I responded.

"Correct," he said. "Validation is challenging for most leaders because many of us believe that our job is to always provide instruction or to come up with solutions. This is not the case. Our job is to listen to employees in order to demonstrate support of their emotional experience. Most managers want to help their employees, but often lack proper validation skills.

"Validation does not mean that we have to agree with how our employee is feeling, but we should acknowledge and accept how they feel. We have to be mindful that employees have a right to feel how they like and it is our job to understand how they feel. Also, we have to be mindful not to minimize how they feel. Feeling strong, sad or angry about something is okay. We have to help them work through their emotions instead of encouraging them to suck it up or get over them. Ignoring how they feel will likely intensify the emotion. Emotions influence behavior, so feelings should be addressed if you desire to understand or change behavior."

"This is so true!" I commented. "Emotions are not about being right or wrong. Emotions typically stem from an individual's perceptions. Rarely if ever do you find two people who think or feel exactly the same. Respecting how people feel is the same as respecting their individuality. This is why it is important to apply skill 2 – Suspend Judgment. I've learned that people will attack when they feel wronged. People will shut down when they feel betrayed, but people will also open up when they feel understood and accepted."

Major Cooked nodded in agreement and said, "You're absolutely right. As managers we must learn to validate and support employees who are in emotional distress. If we validate how they feel, they will be able to work through their emotions much faster. We have to be mindful of how we treat people. One of my favorite quotes that expresses this idea is by Maya Angelou, who said:

'I've learned that
People will forget what you said,
People will forget what you did, but
People will never forget how you made them feel'

"This simple, but powerful quote opened up my eyes to the importance of acknowledging employees' subjective experiences."

"I have never thought about the importance of validating employees' subjective experiences, but this all makes sense," I responded. "If people feel understood, they are more likely to share feelings that might be negatively impacting their morale and performance. The better informed managers are, the better they are equipped to help employees. So, I guess one could argue that by addressing employees' emotional distress, managers can minimize morale and productivity problems."

"Exactly," Major Cook said.

"Why do you talk so passionately about validation?" I inquired.

"Validation minimizes workplace mistrust and strife. Confronted with invalidation, employees will shut down immediately and productivity will likely drop off."

"Also, without comprehension and successful application of this skill, the fifth skill of *Empathic Leadership* cannot be implemented."

"What is Skill 5?" I asked.

"Understanding and implementing Skill 5 is what truly enhances morale and productivity in the workplace and yields the best results for managers. Skill 1 encourages managers to *Lead in a Righteous Manner,* which means to treat their employees justly. Skill 2 encourages managers to *Suspend Judgment,* so that they can recognize and demonstrate appreciation for employees' individuality. Skill 3 encourages managers to *Seek to Understand Employees,* in order to demonstrate compassion for them. Skill 4 encourages managers to *Acknowledge and Validate Subjective Experiences,* in order to help employees feel safe, understood and accepted. Skills 1, 2, 3 and 4 are essential empathy skills that leaders must practice, and yet, they are only building blocks.

"The first four skills are critical to improving morale and productivity in the workplace because they lay the foundation for becoming an *Empathic Leader.* However, without successful implementation of skill 5, managers may not see the boost in morale or productivity that they truly desire."

I looked Major Cook straight in his eyes and asked, "What is Skill 5?"

"Be patient." Major Cook replied. "I will tell you about Skill 5 during our next stop. Skill 5 is what *Empathic Leadership* is all about. Until Skill 5 is implemented, employee morale and productivity will suffer."

"Where are we headed, Sir?"

"The Mental Health Clinic," answered Major Cook. "But before we leave, please take a few minutes to record your thoughts. I want to make sure that you are capturing everything, especially this skill."

I pulled out my pocket recorder and began speaking.

Acknowledge and Validate Subjective Experiences has several benefits:

1. Builds trust between managers and employees
2. Builds genuine relationships
3. Employees feel understood, accepted and cared for
4. Communicates that how employees feel does matter
5. Creates a safe work environment

After I finished recording, Major Cook walked out of the IG office and I followed. As we walked through the long hallway toward the elevator, my curiosity about Skill 5 increased.

I felt my heart rate quicken with anticipation. Thus far, the tour had been a wonderful learning experience. I felt that my leadership style was about to change drastically due to the knowledge that I was acquiring.

We reached the elevator and rode to the first floor. As we exited the elevator, Major Cook and I turned left and walked into the Mental Health Clinic waiting room.

The Mental Health Clinic

Major Cook turned and asked, "Why do you believe that I brought you to the mental health clinic last?"

Not sure what Major Cook was searching for, I replied, "The last shall be first. Sometimes what people need the most is what they often put off until last."

"Correct," responded Major Cook with a smile. "What do people who are experiencing emotional distress normally desire or need the most, but are often reluctant to ask for or seek?"

"Besides validation, I guess *Help?*"

"Exactly!" Major Cook said. "But, do you see any signs on the walls that say that it is okay to get help?"

"No," I replied.

"Why not?"

"When it comes to seeking help we sometimes shame employees for needing assistance. We have even taken drastic measures such as changing the department's name from Mental Health to Behavioral Health in order to minimize the stigma."

"That's so true," Major Cook admitted. "As a society we are conflicted about what it means to seek help. On one hand, we show sympathy and encourage help-seeking behavior so that individuals can get better. On the other hand, we judge individuals and attempt to isolate them because of their distress."

"That's sad, but true," I said. "Unfortunately, we live in a society where seeking help is perceived to be a sign of weakness. For this reason, many individuals avoid seeking help."

"It's not only sad, but discouraging." Major Cook replied. "Although everyone experiences emotional distress at some point in their life, we have a tendency to judge and distance ourselves from those who experience it. Sadly, it is not uncommon for individuals to be labeled 'crazy' for seeking help. There are other reasons that individuals fail to seek help, such as feeling overwhelmed or embarrassed by the problem and denial. The list goes on and on, but the fear of being judged or labeled is the number one reason that prevents employees from seeking help."

"I agree," I said. "We have to rethink how we view and deal with help-seeking behavior. The manner in which individuals behave is typically shaped by the culture in which they work. Unfortunately, due to the recent rise in workplace violence, people who express emotional distress are often treated in a negative manner. They are perceived to be too difficult to work with and sometimes are labeled as being unstable or a danger to themselves and others."

"Exactly," said Major Cook. "In order to resolve this conflict, leaders have to become better informed about the help-seeking process. It is not acceptable to take punitive action against individuals who seek help for emotional distress. I have seen too many individuals be treated unfairly because they had an emotional breakdown at the workplace.

"The most effective way to deal with emotional distress at the workplace is to develop collaborative relationships with employees. Work with employees, not against them. Leaders must allow employees to define their own experience and help them find viable solutions. Collaboration is the key."

"Collaboration?" I repeated.

"Yes, *Maintain a Collaborative Spirit.*"

Smiling, I asked, "What does it involve?"

"The process involves five basic steps," said Major Cook.

"Basic for whom?" I asked with a smirk.

Major Cook laughed. "It's basic for any leader who desires to help employees resolve their emotional distress and find hope in their situation. The steps are fairly simple. First, acknowledge the employee's emotional distress. For example, you can say, 'I am sorry that you feel frustrated.' This will let them know that you are open to talking about how they feel. Second, offer support by asking, 'How can I help you?' This communicates that you are invested in their well-being. Third, provide information about available resources such as Employee Assistance Program (EAP) and Behavioral Health. Fourth, offer words of encouragement such as, 'You will overcome this.' Fifth, confess your approval of help-seeking behavior. For example, you could say, 'I support your decision to seek help and I am willing to escort you if needed.'"

"Why is this skill the most important?" I asked.

"I figured you'd ask that," he said. "As stated previously, *Empathic Leadership* is a process-oriented approach. The primary goal is to identify, discuss and resolve emotional distress that may cause or contribute to low morale and productivity amongst employees. How many times have you heard the sayings, 'Actions speak louder than words' or 'two brains are better than one'?"

He continued, "If you want to truly bond with your employees, help them by offering guidance and aid. Your job as a leader is to make it easy for your employees to do their jobs. If you take care of them, they will take care of the mission. Avoid blaming and isolation! Criticizing your employees' decisions and behavior will often be counterproductive. Collaboration and encouragement, on the other hand, will often promote good behavior, self-confidence and positive emotions. If negative emotions are not resolved, the potential for acting-out, work absences and job dissatisfaction increases."

"I never thought much about helping employees solve their emotional distress," I admitted. "However, I agree that emotions strongly influence behavior. Most people want to be supported when faced with distress."

"Exactly," he said. "Emotional bonding has a greater impact on employees' ability to perform than intellectual bonding. The bonding process between leaders and their employees begins and flourishes as a result of effective collaboration.

"Sir, you have really enlightened me. I have never heard anyone talk so much talk about collaborating with employees. Organizations that operate from a hierarchical approach typically contribute to the belief among leaders that they are too important to collaborate with employees."

Major Cook smiled and said, "Hierarchical authority can create challenges within organizations, but there is nothing wrong with defining and sustaining authority or power boundaries. However, some leaders fail to realize that collaboration is the key to success, not hierarchical authority. Collaboration gives way to better decision-making by employees and increases their personal motivation and problem-solving skills."

As Major Cook finished speaking, I exhaled and thought to myself, *"This makes sense. Collaboration promotes teamwork and empowers employees to take ownership of their emotional distress while also actively participating in problem-solving with leadership."*

Major Cook observed politely and asked, "What are you thinking?"

I looked Major Cook straight in his eyes and said, "Sir, I was just thinking how important it is to not allow power to infer with one's ability to connect with their employees. Several thoughts are racing through my mind because I am extremely excited and encouraged."

With a chuckle, he said, "Don't forget to capture what we have discussed. You have been presented with a lot of information in a short timeframe."

I smiled and thanked him for escorting me through the hospital. As we exited the Mental Health Clinic, I pulled out my pocket recorder and began speaking.

Maintain a Collaborative Spirit has several benefits:

1. Lets employees know that it is okay to ask for support
2. Prevents employees from withdrawing from others
3. Promotes genuine concern for employees and increases loyalty
4. Acknowledges emotional distress as normal
5. Helps the employee to restore a sense of control

After recording my thoughts, I shouted, "This is life-changing information. The tour was awesome! I truly and the importance of practicing the five skills of *Empathic Leaders*."

"Yes, I agree. This information changed my life as well. I am glad that I could share it with you," replied Major Cook. "Let's return to my office. I will share with you the reason I believe that empathic leadership is the most effective management model for enhancing morale and increasing productivity in the workplace."

As we walked toward his office, I continued to reflect on *Empathic Leadership* and the five skills of highly empathic leaders. The five skills are logical and appear to be very straightforward.

Upon entering Major Cooks' office I asked, "What shaped your view of leadership?

Summary of the Five Skills of Highly Empathic Leaders

Lead in a Righteous Manner – encourages leaders to manage employees with integrity, good intentions and dignity.

Suspend Judgment – encourages leaders to monitor their biases and to celebrate individuality.

Seek to Understand Employees – encourages leaders to engage in empathetic listening and to encourage two-way dialogue.

Acknowledge and Validate Subjective Experiences – encourages leaders to validate emotions and show compassion.

Maintain a Collaborative Spirit – encourages leaders to help employees resolve their emotional distress by helping them find hope in their situations.

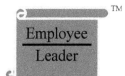 ^{TM}

Leadership Refined

M ajor Cook glanced at me with an eager look and said, "When I first entered the military, I desperately wanted to gain a deeper understanding of what leadership was all about. Like you, I was trained to believe that leadership is an influential interpersonal process that is *all* about motivating people to be productive so that they can accomplish the organization's mission.

"I adopted an autocratic style of leadership. I used control, scare tactics, and a combination of discipline and incentives to motivate employees. I excelled at maintaining order and discipline and as a result, employees knew exactly what was expected of them."

"Did you have any success with this style of leadership?" I asked.

"Some success from a productivity viewpoint, but not much with building morale." Major Cook said. With a disappointed look on his face, he continued, "Practicing an autocratic approach was helpful with clarifying roles, ensuring accountability, meeting short deadlines and achieving results, but it created mistrust and fear amongst my employees."

"Sir, what changed your perspective?" I said.

Major Cook took a book from a bookshelf in the corner of his office. As he set down on the couch across from me, he said, "This book changed my perspective about leadership and laid the foundation for *Empathic Leadership*."

Sensing my surprise, Major Cook quickly said, "I know that you were probably expecting me to tell you that a seasoned and experienced leader changed my perspective. Sorry to disappoint you, but this book did the job."

"What's the name of the book?" I inquired.

"Emotional Intelligence: Why It Can Matter More Than IQ," he said. "The book was published in 1995 by Dr. Daniel Goleman, a prominent psychologist who popularized the concept of Emotional Intelligence."

"Emotional Intelligence, what is that and what does it have to do with being an *Empathic Leader?*" I asked.

"As stated previously, leadership is not just about influencing people so that they can perform well and produce results. Leaders should also be capable of understanding the underlying causes of low morale and productivity. With insight about employees' thoughts and feelings, leaders can assist and provide them with the right resources. This important leadership function requires individuals to possess certain competences and skills that are linked to Emotional Intelligence (EQ).

"In order to become an *Empathic Leader* you must have good intrapersonal and interpersonal skills. Your ability to analyze personal challenges (intrapersonal) within you and social challenges (interpersonal) between you and your employees is essential to becoming an empathic leader. Empathic leadership was birthed out of Goleman's concept of EQ."

"I understand the importance of having good intrapersonal and interpersonal skills," I replied. "How is emotional intelligence defined and what does it involve?"

Glowing as if he were a proud father, he said, "I like the fact that you are an inquisitive young officer. If you continue to seek knowledge you will definitely excel as a leader. Well, according to Dr. Goleman, emotional intelligence is the ability to identify, use, understand, and manage emotions in positive ways to relieve stress, communicate effectively, empathize with others, overcome challenges, and defuse conflict. Dr. Goleman believes that individuals with high emotional intelligence are capable of recognizing their own emotional state and the emotional states of others. This awareness and understanding of emotions helps people better relate to others, form healthier relationships, achieve greater success at work, and lead more fulfilling lives.

"But why, you may ask, are so many leaders like yourself uninformed about emotional intelligence? The answer is simple. Due to the increased pressure on leaders to motivate employees, a large percentage of Chief Executive Officers invest millions of dollars toward the development of administrative and technical skills training programs for leaders. More emphasis is placed on intellectual aptitude and productivity then emotional aptitude and morale. However, this popular, but ineffective, industry practice has been the cause of many failed businesses," said Major Cook.

"So you believe that Chief Executive Officers must redefine what leadership means to their organization by learning about and understanding the concept of emotional intelligence if they are to succeed in today's competitive market?" I inquired.

"Exactly. Over the past few decades, employees have become more assertive about expressing their discontent in the workplace. Given this, leaders must learn to be just as effective in addressing morale issues as they are in addressing productivity issues."

"But how does *Empathic Leadership* align with Emotional Intelligence?" I wondered.

"Oh, let me explain," said Major Cook. "There are four domains to emotional intelligence and domain specific competencies. I keep a handout on my desk to remind me of the four domains. Come over here so I can show you what I am talking about. Look at this."

Emotional Intelligence Outline

Personal Competences

☐ Self-awareness
- The ability to recognize and identify one's emotions, strengths, weaknesses, motives, values and goals. Increased understanding of the cause of emotions and ability to distinguish emotions from actions.

☐ Self-management
- Involves controlling or redirecting one's disruptive emotions and impulses and adapting to changing circumstances.

Social Competences

- Social Awareness **(Empathy)**
    - Sensing others' emotions, understanding their perspective, and taking active interest in their concerns

- Relationship Management
    - Increased ability to analyze and understand relationships
    - Better at problem solving in relationships
    - Ability to motivate, influence, develop, lead and collaborate with others

---

"You see, *Empathic Leadership* aligns with emotional intelligence, with crossover into both personal and social competency areas. After learning about emotional intelligence, I developed *The Empathic Leadership Model*." Major Cook said.

"*The Empathic Leadership Model (ELM)* includes two intrapersonal skills and three interpersonal skills that can be learned and shared with a wide variety of leaders at all levels. The model is designed to facilitate introspection with the intent of increasing social competence in order to develop healthy and empathic relationships in the workplace. Here it is."

Self-Awareness	*Self-Management*	*Social Awareness*	*Relationship Management*
Skill 1 – Lead in a Righteous Manner	*Skill 2 – Suspend Judgment*	*Skill 3 – Seek to Understand Employees* *Skill 4 – Validate*	*Skill 5 – Maintain a Collaborative Spirit*
Aware of values and goals Understand link between feelings, thoughts and behavior Make sound decisions despite uncertainties and pressures	Act ethically Be flexible in how they see events Take fresh perspectives and risks in thinking	Empathize Show sensitivity and understand others' perspectives Attentive to emotional cues and listen well Help out based on understanding	Balance and focus on task with attention to relationships Share information and resources Promote a friendly, cooperative climate Identify and nurture opportunities for collaboration

"Well, now do you understand why organizations must redefine what they consider to be effective leadership?"

"Yes Sir," I responded enthusiastically. "Leadership is about building, nurturing and facilitating healthy and productive relationships in the workplace. Whether leaders like it or not, they must be willing to wear many hats. On any given day, a leader might be viewed as a mental health counselor, an EEO representative or customer service spokesperson."

"Leadership is about motivating employees to achieve a common goal through the **exchange** of mutual respect, compassion and empathy. Leadership is a lead-and-follow process that is designed to create '*Win-Win*' situations for leaders and employees.

"An *Empathic Leader,*" I continued, "is a manager who habitually strives to enhance morale and workplace productivity by gaining a deeper understanding and awareness of employees' thoughts, emotions and perspectives by demonstrating **empathy**.

"The *Empathic Leader* understands that it is impossible to connect with, or influence nyone to perform well; especially employees, if he or she cannot envision what life or work would be like if he or she walked in their shoes. *Empathic leadership* is not dictating at all. It is about creating a positive and compassionate workplace where employees can perform exceptionally well and be their best. Telling employees what to do without considering how they feel or soliciting their input regarding performance improvement is counterproductive. Taking the time to listen and understand employees' emotional disposition is what *Empathic Leadership* is all about."

"I am glad that you understand," said Major Cook. "I had to redefine my leadership style because I was tired of dealing with disgruntled employees who were not performing well because they did not feel valued and respected as human-beings. It was not easy, but I changed my thinking and behavior. If I preached that my employees were my greatest resource than I decided that I had to treat them as such."

After Major Cook finished speaking, I wondered to myself, *"There are many different leadership styles: Servant Leadership, Transformational Leadership, Transactional Leadership and Autocratic Leadership; to name a few, that are taught in academic institutions and training programs around the world because they have been proven to be effective on some level."*

Although Empathic Leadership made sense to me and I realized the importance of applying the *5 Skills of Highly Empathic Leaders*, I turned toward Major Cook and asked my final question. "Sir, considering the various leadership styles why do you believe that *Empathic Leadership* is ideal?"

 ^{TM}

An Effective

Management Model

Smiling warmly, Major Cook replied, "Considering how inquisitive you are, I knew that you would eventually ask this question?" He continued, "There are a number of different leadership styles that are taught in academic institutions and training programs around the world. Each leadership style has its advantages and disadvantages. However, I believe that *Empathic Leadership* is an effective model for enhancing morale and increasing productivity in the workplace because it emphasizes the importance of developing and sustaining healthy and emotionally based relationships in the workplace."

"From personal and professional experience as a leader, I have learned that authoritative tactics and lack of empathy toward employees typically sets the stage for low morale and decreased productivity. In order to achieve long-term success, leaders in every organization must recognize and understand the characteristics of healthy organizational management. Employees play a vital role in influencing and determining workplace productivity, profitability and growth."

"I'm impressed with this leadership style and I am excited about becoming an *Empathic Leader*, but I wonder what kind of results it yields for leaders, employees and the organizations overall." I commented.

"Well, I can only speak about the results that I have personally observed," he said. "By becoming an *Empathic Leader*, I have seen an increase in employee retention, workplace satisfaction, morale and productivity for each of the departments that I have managed over the years."

"Empathic Leadership is an effective management model because the central focus is on creating a healthy organization. Let me show you what the characteristics of a healthy organization are. Pick up that blue folder on my desk and take a look in it."

I did as he said and saw the following:

Characteristics of a Healthy Organization

1.) Productive and Compassionate Employees

Organizational Goal: Recruit and retain high functioning and positive employees who are prepared and ready to accomplish the mission.

Empathic Leadership Objective: Create a positive and compassionate workplace where employees can perform exceptionally well.

Beneficiaries: Leadership and Employees

Effect: Leaders and employees participate in training to enhance emotional intelligence and empathic communication.

2.) Satisfied and Happy Employees

Organizational Goal: Strive to understand and address the psychological needs of all employees.

Empathic Leadership Objective: Strive to gain a deeper understanding and awareness of employees' thoughts, emotions and perspectives by demonstrating empathy.

Beneficiaries: Leadership and Employees

Effect: Employees develop favorable impressions of leaders; communicates that how employees feel does matter.

3.) Valued and Respected Employees

Organizational Goal: Create a harmonious work environment where employees feel that they are the greatest asset to the organization. Employees feel valued and respected. As a result they eagerly engage as a functional team to accomplish the mission.

Empathic Leadership Objective: Develop highly empathic leaders who are capable of achieving the mission by valuing staff, promoting team work and enhancing staff competence.

Beneficiaries: Leadership and Employees

Effect: Staff feel valued, understood, and respected and will embrace the organization's mission. Also, employees will look out for, protect and support their leader in accomplishing the mission.

Then, Major Cook said, "As a leader you must be willing and ready to transform yourself and your organization in order to ensure its success. Taking care of your employees and striving to develop a healthy organization will enable your organization to compete in the marketplace and produce continuous profits. If you desire to achieve and sustain success, be mindful that your organization is only as good as the people who lead it and work in it."

"Sir, I understand and agree with everything that you have shared with me today. I am eager to become an *Empathic Leader*, but I guess I will have to practice the skills in order to become effective in using the approach," I commented.

"Yes, you will need to practice the skills. Believe me, you will have plenty of opportunities. Over time, you will learn for yourself why *Empathic Leadership* is effective," echoed Major Cook. "I look forward to hearing about your future experiences as you strive to become an *Empathic Leader.*"

As I exited Major Cook's office, I said, "Sir, I can't thank you enough for sharing your leadership approach with me. This has been a very enlightening experience and I promise to keep you informed about my journey."

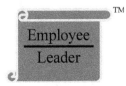

^{TM}

Becoming an Empathic
Leader

Enhancing Morale

After less than a month on the job, Jill entered my office and informed me that she was planning to resign as the Outreach Manager because her husband received short notice relocation orders. She wanted to start preparing for their move to California. Jill informed me that she knew someone who could backfill her position and stated that she would be willing to set up an interview. I thanked her for letting me know about her situation and also providing a potential backfill for her position.

As Jill walked out of my office, I felt disappointment come over me. She was an awesome social worker and very good at her job. She presented well and was very resourceful. Customers loved her.

A few days passed and Jill stopped by my office to drop off the resume of a military spouse, Linda, whom she had met at a Newcomers' Orientation. Jill informed me that she had a brief conversation with Linda after her briefing and felt that Linda would be a good fit for the Outreach Manager position.

After speaking with Jill and reviewing Linda's resume thoroughly, I asked Erica to contact Linda to schedule an interview.

The New Hire

At 0830 hrs on Monday morning, Linda arrived for her interview. As she walked in and introduced herself, I thanked her for considering the position. Immediately after she took her seat, I started the interview by saying, "I reviewed your work experience thoroughly and feel that you are qualified for the job. I am really impressed with your CV and Jill spoke very highly of you. You are hired if you want the job."

With a look of surprise, Linda said, "Yes, I will take the job! I did not expect to find a job so quickly. This is great and I look forward to working with you. What are you looking for in regards to performance?"

"I am looking for someone who is just as good as Jill. She is a great presenter and knows how to engage audiences. Maybe you can get a few pointers from her during the transition so that you can get the same results she received."

Linda thanked me for answering her question and for offering her the position.

Over the course of the interview, I did not ask Linda any questions because I knew what I was looking for and expected. I wanted someone who could perform like Jill. As we approached the end of the interview, I asked, "Do you have any more questions for me Linda?"

Linda replied, "Just one more question, Sir. When would you like me to start working?"

"As soon as possible so that you can have some time to get oriented with Jill."

Linda stood up from her seat and said, "I can start next week if you like."

"Next week is fine! On your way out, please touch base with my assistant, Erica. She will inform you about in-processing requirements."

Linda smiled and said, "Thank you," as she walked out of my office.

Performance Anxiety

Three weeks had passed since Linda started working. According to the feedback that I received from staff and leadership, she was doing a really good job.

Then, to fulfill a training requirement, Linda was asked to give a briefing about the Family Advocacy Program to the entire Medical Group, which consisted of 300 plus employees. I was looking forward to listening to Linda's presentation because I had not yet attended any of her briefings due to my busy schedule.

When the day came, I entered the auditorium and stood in the back. I waved to Linda and flashed her a thumbs up. Linda waved back and returned the gesture.

After everyone was seated, Linda began her presentation. "Good morning, everyone. My name is Linda Jones and I am the Outreach Manager for the Family Advocacy Program. I am here to tell you all about our services."

As I listened, I noticed that Linda's voice was squeaky and then, all of a sudden, she stopped speaking. She glanced into the audience, took a death breath and murmured, "Lt Buckingham can explain more."

I did not understand what was happening with Linda, but I responded quickly by making my way toward the stage to finish the presentation. As I walked on stage, I smiled at Linda and quickly reassured her that everything would be okay. After I finished the presentation, I immediately returned to my office so that I could process what had just occurred. I felt frustrated and thought about reprimanding Linda.

Happy Employee

Thirty minutes later, Linda entered my office and asked if she could speak with me.

"Yes, please have a seat," I replied.

"I apologize about putting you on the spot, but I felt extremely anxious," said Linda.

With a puzzled look I asked, "Anxious about what?"

Hesitating, Linda said, "I felt pressured to perform well and felt nervous about you being in the auditorium. During my interview you consistently reminded me of how good Jill was. You made it very clear that you liked her presentation style and overall work ethic. By the end of the interview I was questioning whether I should take the job. You fixated on Jill's performance capability and work ethic and never gave me the opportunity to share my strengths and weaknesses. I thought to myself, '*I am not Jill. I am different.*'"

She continued, "You need to pay close attention to what you say to people. I was so concerned about pleasing you that I had a short memory lapse. I am so embarrassed about my behavior. I am not sure if I can work under this kind of pressure."

Before responding, I quickly reflected on my time spent with Major Cook and thought about the *5 Skills of Highly Empathic Leaders*. I asked myself, *"What would I like to accomplish from this exchange? This is one of many opportunities that Major Cook mentioned that I would have to practice the Empathic Leadership approach."*

While I was processing my thoughts, Linda waited patiently with an angry look on her face.

I took a deep breath and said, "Thanks for being patient as I gathered my thoughts. I wanted to make sure that I do not respond out of frustration. First, I would like to apologize for placing pressure on you. I did not realize that my words had such an effect on you. It was not my intent to create stress or anxiety for you. I simply wanted you to be just as successful as Jill. I get it now. I would not have responded well either if my boss had compared me to someone else without getting to know me. As I look back on the interview I agree that I did not treat you fairly. For that I am truly sorry. Please forgive me."

Looking stunned, Linda asked, "You are not going to reprimand me for not doing my job and embarrassing you?"

"No," I smiled, "I have to accept responsibility for the way I conducted the interview. It is the right thing to do. I did not inquire about your strengths or weaknesses. I simply bragged about Jill and did not monitor my biases. I failed to suspend judgment and to celebrate your individuality. I will not do this again. I should have treated you in the manner by which you prefer to be treated. However, that did not occur because I never asked you how you prefer to be treated."

Linda smiled at me and said, "I was terrified to come into your office because I knew that you would lecture and reprimand me. I have never worked for a boss who did not respond in a punitive manner if someone did something wrong."

I returned Linda's smile and said, "To be honest, I was angry and was thinking about reprimanding you but, after you shared your perspective about the cause of your performance anxiety, I realized that you were correct. I heard what you said. I am learning to seek understanding so that I can listen in a more compassionate manner. That must have been terrifying and embarrassing for you to be in front of all those people and have a memory lapse."

"Yes, it was very embarrassing," replied Linda. "It felt like my heart was going to explode. It was not a good situation."

"It is normal to feel embarrassed and angry when things do not go as planned. I can definitely relate."

"I did not expect you to validate my feelings by showing compassion or consideration for me after I put you on the spot," Linda said.

"Sometimes we have to step outside of ourselves in order to be available to help others in distress. My natural instinct was to help you. Despite how I felt at the time, I knew I had to get you out of the situation."

Looking directly into my eyes, Linda said, "I think that I am going to like working for you. You believe in taking care of your people."

"Yes, I do," I asserted. "I also believe in maintaining a collaborative spirit. I take pride in inspiring teamwork and empowering my staff by providing guidance and support. Whenever you find yourself in a difficult situation, do not hesitate to ask for assistance. If we are to succeed as a team we have to take care of each other."

By the time we approached the end of our meeting, Linda's emotional disposition had shifted and she appeared to be calm. With a look of appreciation, Linda said, "I like your leadership approach and know that I will perform well under your guidance. I am confident that I will excel working with you. I walked into your office angry and frustrated, but I am walking out feeling very happy."

With humility and gratitude, I thanked Linda for coming to speak with me and said, "No leader can effectively connect with his or her employees without walking in their shoes. As a leader, I can influence morale and productivity. I take full responsibility for my role as a leader. Thanks again."

After processing my meeting with Linda, I realized that I had successfully applied the *5 Skills of Highly Empathic Leaders*. I could not have been more proud of myself. Prior to my time with Major Cook and learning about *Empathic Leadership*, I had been convinced that leadership was all about motivating people to accomplish the mission. However, with my developing knowledge about *Empathic Leadership*, I continued to practice the *5 Skills of Highly Empathic Leaders* on a daily basis. I even wrote an "Empathic Leadership Creed" and had it inscribed on a plaque to remind myself and others of the importance of leading with empathy.

The Empathic Leadership Creed

I _____ will respect my employees and treat them how I desire to be treated.

I will monitor my personal views and biases as I interact with my employees in order to ensure that I respect and celebrate their individuality.

I am responsible for motivating my employees and cannot do so without listening to them and striving to understand their needs, motives and concerns.

I can connect with my employees by normalizing and acknowledging their subjective experiences.

I will make a genuine effort to support and help employees resolve emotional distress by maintaining a collaborative spirit.

I realize that I cannot enhance morale or increase workplace productivity without treating employees with compassion and empathy!

The Big Pay-off – Increasing Workplace Productivity

With less than two months on the job, I saw a significant change in morale and productivity amongst all of my employees. Morale was at an all-time high, which translated into increased productivity (successful management of 225 Exceptional Family Members Program cases, 50 maltreatment cases, 75 overseas clearances and 200 HOMES families). Caseloads were high and our referrals were above average, but my staff gave 100% daily and excelled at taking care of our clients.

Two weeks had passed since my meeting with Linda and everything was going very well. I could not have imagined that things could get any better for my staff or me, but then I received a visit from my squadron commander, Lieutenant Colonel Sarah Greene. As Lt Col Greene entered my office, she informed me that the Joint Commission on Accreditation and Health was coming soon. Anxiously, she said, "This inspection is very important and each service has to do well in order for the hospital to be reaccredited. Can I count on you to do well?"

As I walked from behind my desk to greet Lt Col Greene, I commented, "Ma'am, my staff and I will do well during the inspection because we are clicking on all cylinders and are functioning as a harmonious team."

Smiling, Lt Col Greene said, "Major Cook informed me that you are dedicated to taking care of your people and have begun practicing the *5 Skills of Highly Empathic Leaders*. I was glad to hear this because I know that I can depend on you to come through."

"Yes, Ma'am!" I replied.

After Lt Col Greene left my office, I felt a rush of excitement and apprehension flow through my body at the same time. Excitement rushed through my body as I thought about the inspection as being an opportunity to prove that I am a reliable leader. But as my excitement intensified, so did my concern. My employees were already working long hours to manage heavy caseloads and increased referrals.

While sitting at my desk, I reached for the phone and called Erica into my office. "Will you please schedule a staff meeting as soon as possible?" I asked.

"Yes sir," replied Erica with a puzzled look on her face. "Do you mind if I ask why as soon as possible? Is something wrong, Sir?"

"No, nothing bad from my perspective, but I do not know how the staff will respond to what I need to say to them," I replied.

"Sir, You have dedicated time and energy toward making sure that all staff are respected, valued and understood. Whatever it is that you have to speak with us about, I am pretty sure that everyone will be open and receptive," said Erica.

"Thanks for the kind words and support. I do not mean to sound so alarming, but it is never easy to ask staff to increase their productivity when they are already giving 100%. I do believe that the meeting will go well. I just like to process out loud sometime," I said.

Upon exiting my office Erica turned to me and said, "Sir, I will schedule the meeting for tomorrow at 0800 hrs. Tomorrow is a training day and everyone's schedule is already blocked."

Increasing Workplace Productivity

As Joe, Rhonda, Sara, Linda, Erica, Airman Jackson, Sgt James and TSgt Williams walked into the room at 0745 hrs the following morning and took their seats, I felt slightly nervous. Although we were functioning well as a team, I felt uneasy about the need to ask them to do more.

Before speaking, I looked around the room and out the corner of my right eye, I saw Erica smiling and signaling me to start the meeting. I grinned and started the meeting by saying, "I am somewhat at a loss for words because I have mixed feelings about the need to ask you all to do more. Lt Col Greene stopped by my office the other day and informed me that the Joint Commission is coming soon. Do you all know what the purpose of the Joint Commission is and what a visit means for us?"

Tsgt Williams responded, "Sir, the Joint Commission evaluates and accredits organizations that provide mental health and chemical dependency services. The Joint Commission is responsible for accrediting thousands of behavioral health care organizations under the Comprehensive Accreditation Manual for Behavioral Health Care. Joint Commission accreditation and certification is recognized nationwide as a symbol of quality that reflects an organization's commitment to meeting certain performance standards."

Rhonda added, "A visit from the Joint Commission means more work for us."

"Thanks, both of you are correct," I said. "I welcome the visit because we are doing great work and I am confident that we will succeed as a team. However, I do feel bad about asking you all to increase productivity, especially when you all are already doing so much now.

"I am learning that being a leader is not easy, but it is one of the most rewarding responsibilities that one can have in an organization that believes in providing excellent customer service. My hope is that each of you will view the inspection as an opportunity to showcase the excellent customer service that we provide on a daily basis. With this in mind, I need several individuals to take the lead on a few tasks: 1) conduct record reviews; 2) read all standard operating procedures and update them if warranted; and 3) evaluate training folders for all personnel."

"Sir, when do you need know who is going to do what?" Airman Jackson asked.

"I do not need an answer right now, but wanted to inform you all about the tasks that need to be accomplished."

"I will take the lead on reviewing training folders and will route a sign-up sheet after the meeting," said Erica.

"Thanks, Erica! Teamwork is the best work," I said.

As I scanned the room, no one appeared to be upset or bothered by my request, but I asked, "Does anyone have any concerns or issues that they would like to discuss in regards to my request?"

"Not me," replied Linda. "Personally, I do not mind working harder and longer as long as I know that my efforts are appreciated. You know that I will support you however I can because I believe that you care about us. I am pretty sure that others feel the same as I do."

"Linda is correct," said Joe. "We appreciate you because you always try to give us opportunities to express how we feel. We know that you do not have control over what happens at times, but at the very least you allow us to express our feelings and thoughts."

Rhonda, Sara, Erica, Airman Jackson, Sgt James and TSgt Williams expressed their agreement with Joe by nodding and smiling at me.

"Thanks, I am grateful to have such a wonderful team," I said. "Well, if there is nothing else to discuss, the meeting is adjourned."

Over the next few weeks my staff pulled together and worked very hard and long hours to make sure that we were in good shape for the upcoming Joint Commission inspection. Rhonda, Linda and Joe conducted record reviews, reviewing over 200 records and enthusiastically identified and corrected all inaccuracies. Their thorough review ensured that records were current, accurate and inclusive from first appointment to closure.

TSgt Williams, Sgt James and Airman Jackson read through 12 standard operating procedures and revised 5 policies, thus ensuring 100% compliance with the Joint Commission performance standards.

Erica and Sara, meanwhile, evaluated personnel training folders and ensured that each section of the training folders were complete. They created a checklist for each employee to make sure that all training folders adhered to standards. Ultimately, everyone pitched in and worked diligently to maximize compliance with JC standards. We even had working luncheons and everyone volunteered to come in over the weekends if warranted. I was truly impressed with their teamwork and enthusiasm.

The Inspection

Two months had passed since we received the notice that the Joint Commission was coming. As a result of my dedicated and harmonious team, the Family Advocacy Program was in top-notch condition for the inspection.

On one very calm Monday morning in December, Major Cook walked into my office and informed me that the Joint Commission surveyors would be arriving on Wednesday and were scheduled to meet with my team on Friday at 0900 hrs. "You can select up to five records that you want the surveyors to review," he added. "They will thoroughly review each record and can potentially request to see more. Also, be prepared to answer patient safety and customer service questions."

I replied, "Sir, thanks for the update and brief overview of the rules of engagement."

After walking with Major Cook to the front office exit, I returned to my computer and sent the following email:

Dear Team,

The time has come for us to showcase our talent. Major Cook just informed me that the inspection surveyors will be in our area on Friday morning at 0900 hrs. As stated previously, I am confident that we will succeed and thank all of you for making sure that we excel. Please have a brief meeting and select five records that you all think I should share with the surveyors. Also, be prepared to answer questions about patient safety and customer service.

Show the surveyors what you are made of and believe me they will be impressed like I am on a daily basis. Do not hesitate to stop by my office with questions or concerns.

Thanks in advance,

Lt Buckingham
Family Advocacy Officer

Friday morning rolled around quickly and I found myself seated in our meeting room with three surveyors for an extended period of time. Just as Major Cook mentioned, they reviewed each record thoroughly and asked several questions about patient safety and customer service. I maintained my composure and answered all of their questions in a very calm manner. Three hours later, the record review and questioning had come to an end.

Curious, I asked, "How did we do?"

One of the surveyors turned toward me and said, "We will provide a detailed report to your leadership, but I can say that I am very impressed with how you are managing this program."

I thanked the surveyor and asked, "What else would you all like to know about my program?"

"Where do you keep your records and training folders?" asked one of the surveyors.

"Our records are stored in the front office. Would you like to see them?" I asked.

"Yes, that would be nice."

I walked the surveyors to the front office where records are kept in a locked file cabinet. As we entered the front office Erica said, "Good afternoon! How can I help?" with an energetic and enthusiastic smile.

Erica was asked to provide training folders for all staff and she gladly complied. After securing the folders, Erica escorted the surveyors to Sara's office, where they spent an hour with Erica and Sara reviewing and discussing training standards. After meeting with Erica and Sara the surveyors were escorted back to my office. Upon entering my office, they informed me that their inspection was complete. I thanked each of them for giving us the opportunity to share information about our program.

The Out Brief with Hospital Leadership

Two days after meeting with my team, the surveyors had completed their inspection. Over 200 senior leaders and managers from all levels gathered in the auditorium to hear the final results. As one of the surveyors approached the podium to speak, everyone stopped talking and auditorium was filled with silence. The surveyor enlarged his PowerPoint presentation and began speaking, "As you all know, our mission is to continuously improve health care for the public, in collaboration with other stakeholders, by evaluating health care organizations and inspiring them to excel in providing safe and effective care of the highest quality and value.

"During our time at the 325th Fighter Wing, we have met some very dedicated individuals who work hard to provide safe and customer friendly service with the highest quality. We inspected several areas and were very impressed with several programs. The Family Advocacy Program and the Mental Health Clinic were only two of six areas that received a 100% compliance rating. Given this, I am proud to announce that we will be recommending reaccreditation for the hospital."

At the end of the surveyor's brief, the hospital commander thanked him and announced that there would be a celebration for all personnel next week. He said, "I am extremely proud of the work that is being done under my leadership. I am honored to work and serve with such a competent and dedicated group of individuals. Take some time to take care of yourselves and pat yourselves on the back for job well done. Have a good day!"

The Joint Commission Recognition Celebration

The following week, over 120 personnel gathered in the picnic area to celebrate the hospital's accomplishment.

As Ltc Greene took center stage to kick off the celebration, she turned to me and signaled me and my staff to walk toward the front. After my staff and I were front and center, Ltc Greene began, "I cannot express how proud I am of each and every one of you. Because of your hard work, dedication and competence, we met accreditation standards with flying colors. Everyone worked as a team and got the job done. I am overwhelmed with gratitude, but want to remind you all that this gathering is not just about celebrating our accomplishment; it is about recognizing and taking care of people. Each service did an outstanding job and I am very proud of everyone. We have some outstanding young leaders among us and I would like to publicly recognize one of them. Lt Buckingham was singled out during the Joint Commission visit as an exemplary and impressive young officer and was praised by surveyors for his flawless program, 100% compliance score and dedication to building team spirit.

"Surveyors also reported how high-spirited and energetic Lt Buckingham's team was during their interviews. Feedback from the surveyors reflects Lt Buckingham's dedication to achieving the mission. It also reflects his dedication to taking care of his staff. In recognition of his program's success, Lt Buckingham will be nominated for Company Grade Officer of the quarter and each one of his eligible employees will receive financial bonuses for their outstanding performance.

"As we celebrate our accomplishment, I would like to remind all leaders to please continue to take care of yourselves and your employees. If you do these two things, we will have many more celebrations. Thanks again, enjoy the food and have a wonderful day!"

After enjoying quality time with my staff at the celebration, I returned to my office so that I could reflect on the growth and success that I had experienced as a result of practicing the *5 Skills of Highly Empathic Leaders*. As I sat quietly, I was filled with pride because I knew that I had evolved into an *Empathic Leader*.

Remembering my promise to keep Major Cook informed of my journey, I called and asked if I could pay him a follow up visit. He agreed. As I headed to Major Cook's office, I could not wait to find out if he would agree that I had evolved into an *Empathic Leader*.

I believed that I had become an *Empathic Leader* because my staff felt valued, respected and understood. *"But what would Major Cook think?"* I wondered.

The New Empathic Leader

Major Cook greeted me at the door and welcomed me to come in to have a seat. "So how was your journey?" he asked.

"I have learned a great deal about leadership in a very short time period. I believe beyond doubt that *Empathic Leadership* is one of the most effective management models for enhancing morale and increasing productivity. I have observed a significant change in my staff's morale level and productivity. They willingly go above and beyond to achieve the mission. I believe that this change occurred partially because I make a conscious effort to demonstrate empathy as I interact with them. Applying the *5 Skills of Highly Empathic Leaders* really works. I am amazed about how productivity increases when employees feel respected, understood and valued."

"I am glad," Major Cook stated. "I am pretty sure you would like to know if I think that you have evolved into being an *Empathic Leader*."

"How did you know?" I asked.

"Well, I have learned that most people like to receive feedback when they have been tasked or challenged to do something. Considering how inquisitive you are, I knew that you would want to know my thoughts."

"That's interesting," I replied.

Smiling, Major Cook said, "It does not matter whether or not I believe that you have become an *Empathic Leader*. I do not have the authority to decide who successfully becomes an *Empathic Leader*."

"What do you mean?"

"Well it is very simple, Lt Buckingham. Your employees decide, not me," responded Major Cook. "We all like to believe that we are *Empathic Leaders*, but the proof is in how our employees view us. You can determine if you have become an *Empathic Leader* by listening to feedback that you receive from your employees."

Nodding in agreement, I replied, "Sir, you are absolutely correct. I felt that I had become an *Empathic Leader* prior to coming to your office because my employees have repeatedly confirmed my belief. However, I was looking for approval from you. I guess I am looking in the wrong place."

"You got it!" he said. "When your employees believe that you can relate to them, that you care about them and are compassionate toward them, it is then, and only then, you have become an *Empathic Leader*.

"Now if you want to know what I think about you personally, I will share my thoughts." Major Cook commented. "I personally believe that you have become an *Empathic Leader* because several of your staff members have stopped by my office on numerous occasions and bragged about your leadership style. They reported that you are open-minded, fair and easy to work with. They also reported that you are dedicated to taking care of people as well as achieving the mission. As I allowed each of them to voice their opinion of you, they raved about how compassionate and considerate you are as a leader. When I asked each of them to provide me with one word to describe your leadership style, they all said 'empathic.'"

As I processed that, I realized that I had become an *Empathic Leader*, but not because I believed it and not because Major Cook believed it, but because I had invested time in developing healthy relationships with my employees by leading in a righteous manner, suspending judgment, seeking to understand, acknowledging subjective experiences and maintaining a collaborative spirit."

I felt good about becoming an *Empathic Leader* and thanked Major Cook for helping me to evolve. As I rose to leave, he said, "Remember that morale and productivity are interrelated and should always be addressed simultaneously. As you move up in the ranking structure and mentor junior officers, please remind them that empathy is an indispensable leadership skill that is needed to enhance morale and increase productivity."

"I most definitely will Sir," I replied enthusiastically.

Organizational Training

Course: Empathic Leadership

Empathic Leadership is an interpersonal skills development course designed to teach leaders The 5 Skills of Highly Empathic Leaders in order to enhance morale and increase productivity in the workplace. Through a process oriented cognitive-behavioral curriculum, leaders will learn how to apply The 5 Skills of Highly Empathic Leaders and gain a deeper understanding of how to help their employees to be their best by creating a safe, compassionate and harmonious work environment where they can perform exceptionally well.

Course Description:

Participants are introduced to the concept of empathy, including the 5 Skills of Highly Empathic Leaders, and learn why becoming an empathic leader is required if they desire to transform and advance their organizations within their competitive markets. Various leadership styles are discussed and participants learn how to recognize ineffective leadership approaches. Participants receive instructor and peer feedback in a safe and compassionate manner and are instructed to replicate the behavior throughout the course.

Course Goals:

At the end of the program, leaders will be able to:
- Better understand how to manage employees with integrity, good intent and dignity

- Identify and monitor personal biases that negatively impact their ability to celebrate individuality in the workplace

- Verbalize the importance of engaging in empathic listening and two-way dialogue

- Explain why validation and compassion can help leaders align with their employees

- Describe the benefits of maintaining a collaborative spirit with their employees

- Apply all 5 skills and articulate why empathic leadership can no longer be optional

Target Audience:

- Chief Executive Officers
- Management & Leadership at All Levels
- Customer Service Personnel
- Human Resource Staff

Organizational Benefits:

The 5 Skills of Highly Empathic Leaders are indispensable life skills that can help any leader transform his or her work environment into a safe, productive, profitable, compassionate and successful place to work. Participation in this training program will result in:

- Highly empathic leaders
- Motivated and inspired employees
- Increased retention rates
- Increased employee workplace satisfaction
- Enhanced morale
- Increased productivity

All participants will gain a renewed commitment to achieving the organization's mission with compassion and enthusiasm.

Required Training Material:

1. **The Empathic Leader Workbook,** which contains the following handouts:

- Empathic Leadership Pre-Test
- Identification of Emotions
- Emotional Regulation
- Self-scoring Leadership Style Test
- Empathic Leadership is about Getting to Know Your Employees
- Empathic Leadership Self-Survey
- Empathic Leadership Post-Test

2. **"The Empathic Leader: An Effective Management Model for Enhancing Morale and Increasing Productivity"** – book authored by Dr. Dwayne L. Buckingham, which provides information about the origination of empathic leadership.

Course Duration: 8 hour, all-day workshop

For more information about Dr. Dwayne L. Buckingham and his availability for presenting keynotes and seminars, please contact him at: dwayne@realhorizonsdlbcom or

RHCS
P.O. Box 2665
Silver Spring, MD 20915
240-242-4087 Voice Mail
www.realhorizonsdlb.com

Acknowledgments

Over the past fifteen years as a psychotherapist, military officer and human relations consultant, I have had the wonderful opportunity of working with thousands of leaders and employees. Many people have made contributions to this book, and I would like to extend special appreciation to those who provided a wealth of information that laid the foundation for this book.

I would also like to thank Colonel David Hamilton of the United States Air Force for his leadership and guidance in helping me understand the importance of establishing empathic relationships with employees. As my first supervisor in the military, he took the time to hear me out and taught me that organizational success is determined by the quality of relationships between leaders and employees. He made it easy to come to work and motivated me to excel in the workplace.

The leadership and consultative opportunities at Walter Reed National Military Medical Center (WRNMMC) have been very rewarding over the past four years. As a service chief, I have received outstanding support from senior executive officers. Sincere appreciation is extended to CAPT John Ralph, Colonel Deborah Dunivian, Colonel Brett Schenider, CDR James West and CDR Russell Carr. I am forever grateful.

About the Author

Dwayne L. Buckingham, Ph.D, LCSW, BCD is a military veteran who spent more than a decade in the United States Air Force as a commissioned officer and clinician providing psychological assessments, treatment, psycho-educational training and consultation to over 40,000 military personnel and other eligible beneficiaries worldwide. In recognition of his outstanding service, Dr. Buckingham received six Commendation medals, a National Defense Service Medal, a Global War on Terrorism Service Medal and five Achievement/Unit Medals.

Currently, Dr. Buckingham is commissioned as an active duty Commander in the United States Public Health Service and is detailed to Walter Reed National Military Medical Center located in Bethesda, Maryland. Dr. Buckingham is well respected among his professional colleagues and is known as "The Empathy and Resiliency Doctor or The E.R. Doctor".

He is President and Chief Executive Officer of R.E.A.L. Horizons Consulting Service, a human service consulting firm that specializes in providing high-quality coaching, education, training, speaking and facilitation services to individuals, couples, nonprofit organizations, small businesses, Fortune 500 companies, healthcare organizations and human service agencies. His firm has an excellent reputation for helping individuals and organizations resolve challenges that impede productivity and growth.

Dr. Buckingham holds a B.S.W. in Social Work from Jackson State University, a M.S.W in Clinical Social Work from Michigan State University, a Ph.D. in Human Services from Capella University and is Board Certified by the American Board of Examiners in Clinical Social Work. He is a highly sought-after professional speaker, author, film producer, seminar facilitator and consultant. He is also an active member of the National Association of Social Workers and Kappa Alpha Psi Fraternity, Inc.

103

WITHDRAWN

CPSIA information can be obtained
at www.ICGtesting.com
Printed in the USA
LVHW040839281018
595120LV00002B/208/P